For Ed, who always believed I could do this and helped make it happen.—S. R.

For family and friends, who supported me and believed in my drawings from the beginning.—Ezequiel Decarli

First published 2019 by Peacock Press
www.SusanRobinsonAuthor.com
Printed in the U.S.A.

10 9 8 7 6 5 4 3 2 1

Copyright © 2019 by Susan Robinson

All rights reserved. No part of this book may be reproduced, transmitted or stored in an information retrieval system in any form or by any means, graphic, electronic or mechanical, including photocopying, taping and recording, without prior permission from the publisher, except by a reviewer who may quote brief passages in a review.

ISBN 978-1-7335067-0-0

WHEN POKE WOKE

BY SUSAN ROBINSON

ILLUSTRATED BY
EZEQUIEL DECARLI

Peacock Press
Hockessin, Delaware

BAM! Old Man Grizzleface's screen door smacked open. Teeth bared, The Mangy Mongrel kicked up dirt and barreled through the broken gate.

WOOF! WOOF!

Ziggy the rabbit zigzagged across the meadow and ducked into her burrow. Dash the squirrel flung his nuts into the air and scampered up a walnut tree. Poke the hedgehog dropped his blackberries, tucked his chin, and rolled into a ball.

The Mangy Mongrel ranged around the meadow.
"Get back here, you mangy mongrel!" yelled Old Man Grizzleface.
The Mangy Mongrel snorted and trotted back to the house, his tail drooping.

SNIIIIFF!

Ziggy and Dash stomped and frowned at Poke.

"Scaredy-cat!" said Ziggy. "Why didn't you hop? It's brave to zigzag through the grass with The Mangy Mongrel nipping at your cottontail."

"Party pooper!" said Dash. "Why didn't you run? It's fun to scamper up a tree and swish your furry tail at The Mangy Mongrel."

Poke hung his head. Ziggy and Dash run and hop when The Mangy Mongrel chases them, he thought. They are fearless and they have fun. Why do I have spines? Why can't I race like my friends?

He gathered his berries. Dash sprints all the time. Maybe I just need to practice.

Suddenly Poke smelled something sweet. He followed the scent to a chunk of honeycomb beneath the maple tree. MMMM! He stuck in his snout.

Angry bees chased him as he sprinted home to the hedgerow, where he licked his stings and curled into a ball.

On Thursday the friends fished for minnows in the creek. Then Poke twirled Ziggy and Dash, sending them careening, and they pretended to freeze into silly statues.

"WHEE! Look at me!" said Ziggy. "I'm Old Man Grizzleface!"
"WHEE! Look at me!" said Dash. "I'm The Mangy Mongrel!"

GROWL! Poke's tummy announced lunch. Poke and Ziggy picked sunflowers and flicked the seeds into their mouths. Dash peeled away a chestnut burr and nibbled on the nut. The friends crunched until their bellies bulged.

Poke burped, and his spines stood on end.

"Poke's a chestnut!" said Dash. He and Ziggy laughed and pointed. They flopped on their backs, sunbathing on the creek bank, Dash cradling an armful of chestnuts. Poke hung his head and crawled under a beech tree. Rolling into a ball, he snored. SKKZZXX!

BURP!

BAM! Old Man Grizzleface's screen door smacked open. Teeth bared, The Mangy Mongrel kicked up dirt and barreled through the broken gate.

The friends sprang up. Ziggy zigzagged across the creek toward her burrow. Dash scampered to the chestnut tree. Poke hugged his sunflower to his chest and tucked his chin.

No! he thought. If I can't run, I'll hop like Ziggy.

He flung his flower into the air and hopped through the Queen Anne's lace.

The Mangy Mongrel closed in.

Poke couldn't zigzag to the tunnel in time like Ziggy. He couldn't scamper to a tree as quickly as Dash. The Mangy Mongrel's breath steamed on Poke's neck as his jaws snapped at Poke's back.

YELP! YOWL!

Pawing at his face, The Mangy Mongrel snorted and slunk back to the house, his tail drooping.

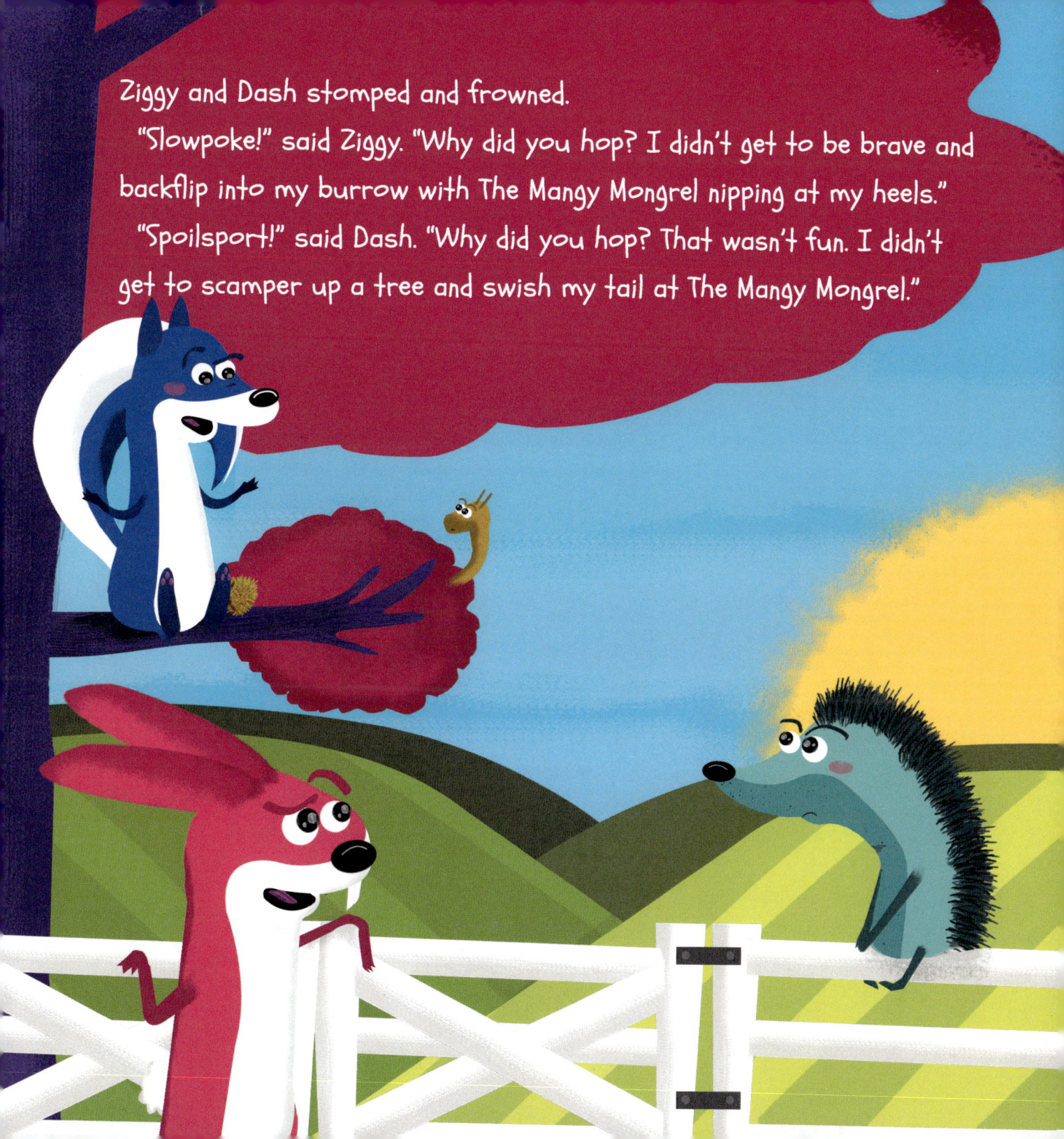

Ziggy and Dash stomped and frowned.

"Slowpoke!" said Ziggy. "Why did you hop? I didn't get to be brave and backflip into my burrow with The Mangy Mongrel nipping at my heels."

"Spoilsport!" said Dash. "Why did you hop? That wasn't fun. I didn't get to scamper up a tree and swish my tail at The Mangy Mongrel."

Hanging his head like his sunflower, Poke trudged home. *Ziggy hops all the time. Maybe I just need to practice.*

Lost in thought, Poke tripped over a turtle making her way to the creek. Rubbing his knee, Poke hopped all the way home to the hedgerow. Then he limped to bed, curling into a ball.

On Friday, Ziggy didn't want to play after lunch. She yawned. "Let's just take a nap." Nestled in a grotto, the animals stretched out, with Poke in the middle. Ziggy and Dash snored. SKKZZXX!

But a stone jabbed Poke's back. He rolled onto his belly. He twisted to one side and then the other. His friends yelled when Poke's spines stabbed them.

So Poke tiptoed away, curling into a ball under a creeping willow.
  Poke dreamed it was his birthday and his friends had made him a grub and beetle cake. MMMM! Just as he dug in, The Mangy Mongrel barged through the boxwood, baring his teeth and snarling. GRRRR!

Poke's eyes fluttered open. What a nightmare! Then his eyes widened. On a rock above Ziggy and Dash, teeth bared and gums gleaming, crouched The Mangy Mongrel!

Ziggy and Dash woke and froze like statues. The Mangy Mongrel leapt toward them.

Poke jumped up, skittered in front of his friends, and rolled into a ball. Eyes bulging, The Mangy Mongrel skidded to a stop and bolted back to the house, his tail drooping.

Poke unrolled. Ziggy and Dash clapped and danced.

"Hero dear-o!" said Ziggy. "You saved us! Thank you for rolling into a ball."

"Fearless friend!" said Dash. "Thank you for sticking out your spines. Was it fun?"

Poke smoothed his spines. "It will be fun to play with my friends." He tapped Ziggy's shoulder. "Tag! You're it!"

"Smiley spiny!" said Ziggy. "We can't tag you."

"Nutty buddy!" said Dash. "We'd run home yelping and yowling like The Mangy Mongrel."

They all laughed. Poke smiled and waddled home. Curling into a ball under the hedgerow, he dreamed of a grub and beetle cake.

Susan Robinson fell in love with picture books as a mom, teacher of the gifted, and school librarian.

She fell in love with hedgehogs when a wildlife rehabilitator brought one to her class. Now she indulges her passions by creating character voices when she reads—sometimes about hedgehogs—to her grandchildren.

Ezequiel Decarli began drawing as a child. He spent entire days making up stories and filling notebooks and odd scraps of paper with real and make-believe characters.

When he grew up, the demands of life intruded, and he put away his pens and paper. However, that love of drawing remained latent, and he finally realized his passion through a career as a graphic designer and illustrator.

Made in the USA
Middletown, DE
10 June 2019